DINOSAUR PROFILES

VELOCIRAPTOR

Titles in the Dinosaur Profiles series include:

DINOSAUR PROFILES

VELOCIRAPTOR

Text by Fabio Marco Dalla Vecchia
Illustrations by Leonello Calvetti and Luca Massini

BLACKBIRCH PRESS
An imprint of Thomson Gale, a part of The Thomson Corporation

THOMSON
™
GALE

Detroit • New York • San Francisco • New Haven, Conn. • Waterville, Maine • London

Computer illustrations 3D and 2D: Leonello Calvetti and Luca Massini

Photographs: page 21, Louie Psihoyos/CORBIS

LIBRARY OF CONGRESS CATALOGING-IN-PUBLICATION DATA

Dalla Vecchia, Fabio Marco.
Velociraptor / text by Fabio Marco Dalla Vecchia ; illustrations by Leonello Calvetti and Luca Massini.
    p. cm.—(Dinosaur profiles)
Includes bibliographical references and index.
ISBN-13: 978-1-4103-0737-8 (hardcover)
ISBN-10: 1-4103-0737-9 (hardcover)
1. Velociraptor—Juvenile literature. I. Calvetti, Leonello, ill. II. Massini, Luca, ill. III. Title.

QE862.S3D435 2007
567.912—dc22
                                                                    2007002028

CONTENTS

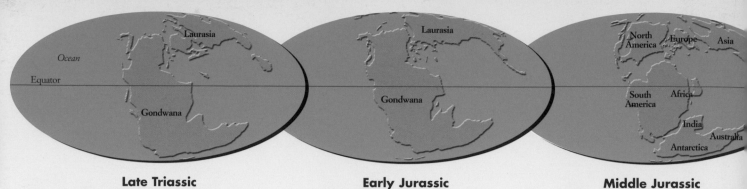

Late Triassic
228–206 million years ago

Early Jurassic
206–176 million years ago

Middle Jurassic
176–161 million years ago

A CHANGING WORLD

Earth's long history began 4.6 billion years ago. Dinosaurs are some of the most fascinating animals from the planet's long past.

The word *dinosaur* comes from the word *dinosauria*. This word was invented by the English scientist Richard Owen in 1842. It comes from two Greek words, *deinos* and *sauros*. Together, these words mean "terrifying lizards."

The dinosaur era, also called the Mesozoic era, lasted from 228 million years ago to 65 million years ago. It is divided into three periods. The first, the Triassic period, lasted 42 million years. The second, the Jurassic period, lasted 61 million years. The third, the Cretaceous period, lasted 79 million years. Dinosaurs ruled the world for a huge time span of 160 million years.

Like dinosaurs, mammals appeared at the end of the Triassic period. During the time of dinosaurs, mammals were small animals the size of a mouse. Only after dinosaurs became extinct did

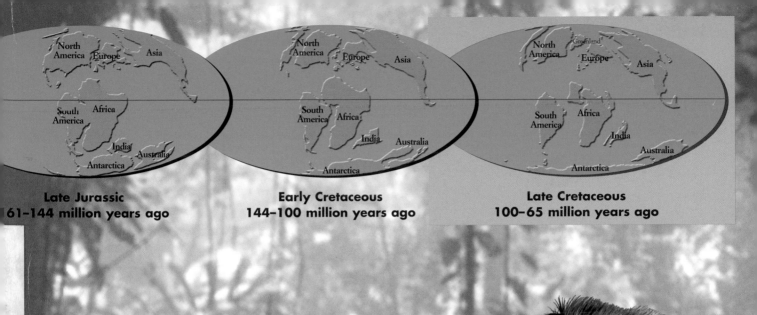

Late Jurassic
61–144 million years ago

Early Cretaceous
144–100 million years ago

Late Cretaceous
100–65 million years ago

mammals develop into the many forms that exist today. Humans never met Mesozoic dinosaurs. The dinosaurs were gone nearly 65 million years before humans appeared on Earth.

Dinosaurs changed in time. Stegosaurus and Brachiosaurus no longer existed when Tyrannosaurus and Triceratops appeared 75 million years later.

The dinosaur world was different from today's world. The climate was warmer, with few extremes. The position of the continents was different. Plants were constantly changing, and grass did not even exist.

7

A Speedy Hunter

The name *Velociraptor* comes from Latin and means "swift raptor." A raptor is a bird that preys on animals and other birds. Velociraptor was not very big. It was only about 6 feet (2m) long and weighed about 22 to 33 pounds (10 to 15 kg).

Even though Velociraptor was small, it was a skillful predator. It had a large claw similar to those of modern-day raptors such as owls, falcons, and eagles. It could move quickly and nimbly because its skeleton was lightweight. These features allowed it to catch and kill prey easily.

Velociraptor lived around 75 million years ago. Its closest relatives are the members of the Dromeosauridae family. This family includes Deinonychus and Dromeosaurus. Many paleontologists (scientists who study dinosaurs) believe dromeosaurids were the cousins of today's birds.

Velociraptor lived in central Asia. Its remains have been discovered in the Gobi Desert in Mongolia and China.

SIBERIA

Ulan Bator

Beijing

This map with modern cities shows
northern Mongolia during the late
Cretaceous period. The brown areas
show mountains. The red dot shows
one place where Velociraptor fossils
have been discovered.

Velociraptor Eggs

Because it lived in the harsh desert, Velociraptor had to be very careful when choosing a place to build a nest and lay eggs. The nest had to be in a shady place, out of the hot sun. It also had to be in a place that was protected from fierce sandstorms.

There were other dangers to the eggs as well. Many desert animals, such as small mammals and large lizards, rested in the shade during the day. At night, these animals came out and sometimes tried to raid the nests.

YOUNG HUNTERS

Velociraptors, especially young ones, were too small to hunt larger dinosaurs. So they preyed on smaller animals. These included mammals, such as mice and shrews, and small reptiles. Velociraptors hunted alone, not in packs as some other dinosaurs did.

Were They Warm-Blooded?

Paleontologists once thought that all dinosaurs were cold-blooded, like lizards and crocodiles. The body temperature of cold-blooded animals depends on the outside temperature around them. Most cold-blooded animals cannot move very quickly when it is cold.

The discovery of Velociraptor—who could move speedily—helped change this view. Today paleontologists think these dinosaurs and their relatives were warm-blooded, like modern-day birds. Some of them may have even had feathers, which helped hold in body heat.

In 1971, the skeletons of a Velociraptor and a Protoceratops clutching each other were found in rocks that were once ancient sand dunes. Protoceratops was a squat dinosaur as large as a hog. It had a beak like a parrot's and a bone frill that protected its neck. It ate plants and was very common in the area where Velociraptor lived.

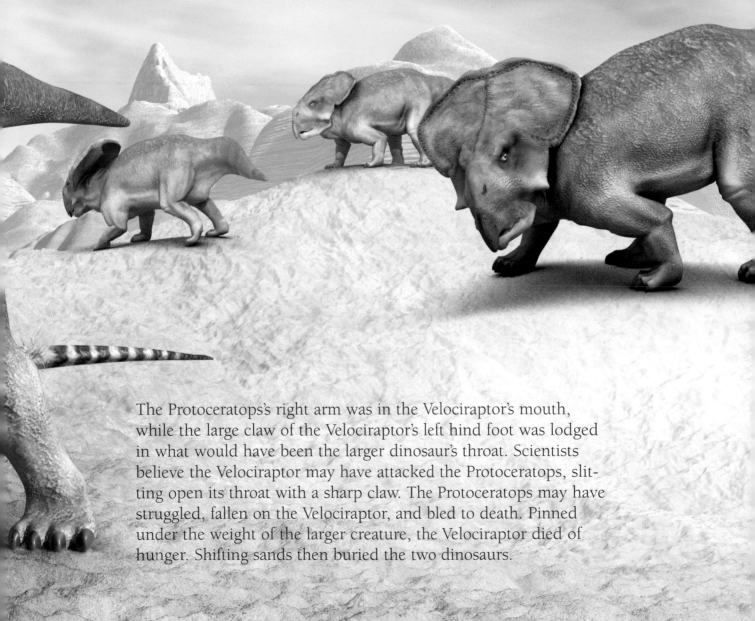

The Protoceratops's right arm was in the Velociraptor's mouth, while the large claw of the Velociraptor's left hind foot was lodged in what would have been the larger dinosaur's throat. Scientists believe the Velociraptor may have attacked the Protoceratops, slitting open its throat with a sharp claw. The Protoceratops may have struggled, fallen on the Velociraptor, and bled to death. Pinned under the weight of the larger creature, the Velociraptor died of hunger. Shifting sands then buried the two dinosaurs.

THE VELOCIRAPTOR BODY

The Velociraptor skull was less than 8 inches (20cm) long. It had a long snout and large orbits (eye holes). The jaw had curved and jagged teeth. There were 28 teeth in the lower jaw and 30 in the upper jaw.

orbit

nostril

dorsal vertebra

cervical vertebra

scapula

lower jaw

hand

rib

tibia

femur

foot

The Velociraptor skeleton was light because the bones were slender and hollow. The long tail was made stiff by bundles of thin, bony rods. The sharp claw on the inner toe of the hind foot was large and shaped like a crescent.

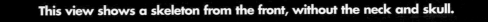

This view shows a skeleton from the front, without the neck and skull.

Scientists believe that Velociraptor used this claw as a
weapon to slash open the belly or throat of the dinosaurs
that it hunted for food. Or it may have used the claw to
kill any animal that passed close by. Another idea is that
the Velociraptor used the claw to climb onto the back of its
prey and kill it more easily.

caudal
vertebra

bony rods

crescent-shaped
first toe

big toe

This view shows a skeleton from above.

Digging Up Velociraptor

More than a dozen Velociraptor fossils have been found. They consist of partial skeletons and skulls of both adults and younger dinosaurs. The first skull complete with jawbones was found in 1923 in the Gobi Desert.

In the movie *Jurassic Park,* the ferocious bipedal dinosaurs that roam in packs are called raptors. But they are not Velociraptors. They are much larger and look more like Deinonychus, which lived in what is now the Americas.

The oldest relative of the Velociraptor was found in China. It is known as Microraptor. What made this discovery so exciting was that Microraptor had feathers. As a result, many scientists now believe that Velociraptor most likely had feathers, too. But no Velociraptor fossils with feathers have been found.

This famous fossil is of a Velociraptor and a Protoceratops clutching each other. It is on display in Ulan Bator, in Mongolia.

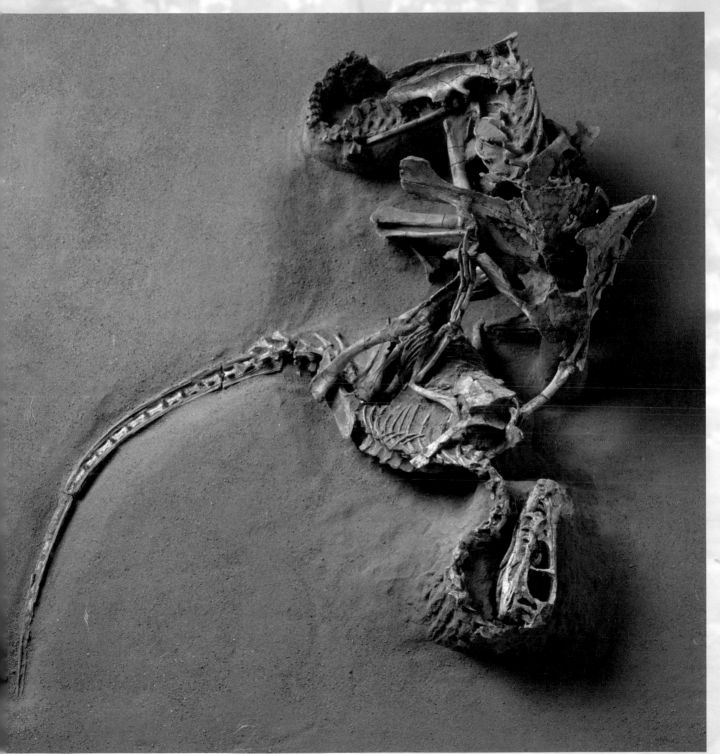

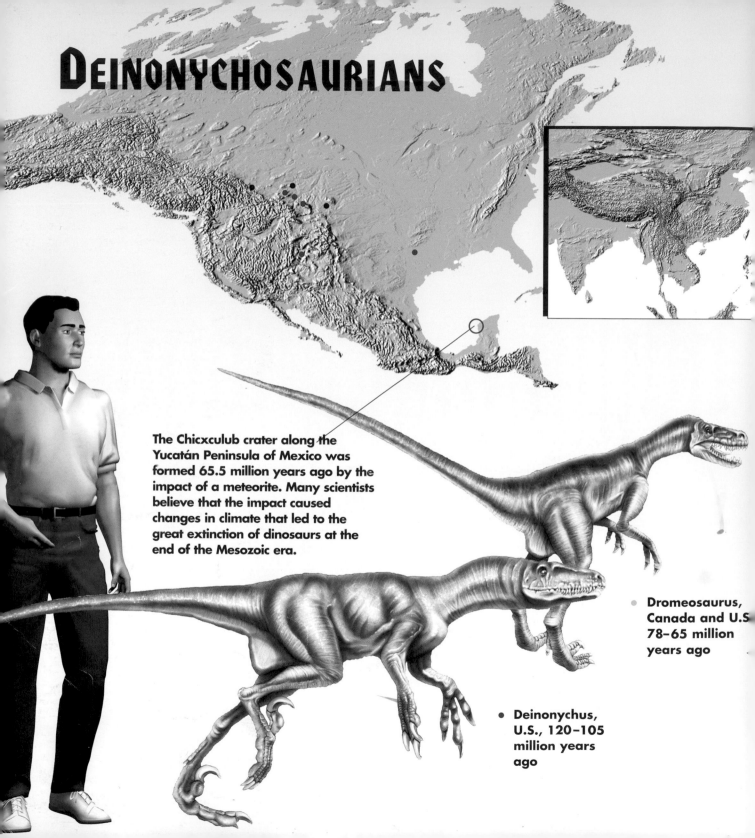

DEINONYCHOSAURIANS

The Chicxculub crater along the Yucatán Peninsula of Mexico was formed 65.5 million years ago by the impact of a meteorite. Many scientists believe that the impact caused changes in climate that led to the great extinction of dinosaurs at the end of the Mesozoic era.

- Dromeosaurus, Canada and U.S 78–65 million years ago

- Deinonychus, U.S., 120–105 million years ago

THE GREAT EXTINCTION

Sixty-five million years ago, dinosaurs became extinct. This may have happened because a large meteorite struck Earth. A wide crater caused by a meteorite 65 million years ago has been located along the coast of the Yucatán Peninsula in Mexico. The impact of the meteorite would have produced an enormous amount of dust. This dust would have stayed suspended in the atmosphere and blocked sunlight for a long time. A lack of sunlight would have caused a drastic drop in Earth's temperature and killed plants. The plant-eating dinosaurs would have died, starved and frozen. As a result, meat-eating dinosaurs would have had no prey and would also have starved.

Some scientists believe dinosaurs did not die out completely. They think that birds were feathered dinosaurs that survived the great extinction. That would make the present-day chicken and all of its feathered relatives descendants of the large dinosaurs.

Opposite: This map shows sites where the deinonychosaurians pictured below have been found.

Troodon, U.S. and Canada, 78–65 million years ago

● Velociraptor, Mongolia, 80–70 million years ago

THE EVOLUTION OF DINOSAURS

The oldest dinosaur fossils are 220–225 million years old and have been found mainly in South America. They have also been found in Africa, India, and North America. Dinosaurs probably evolved from small and nimble bipedal reptiles like the Triassic Lagosuchus of Argentina. Dinosaurs were able to rule the world because their legs were held directly under the body, like those of modern mammals. This made them faster and less clumsy than other reptiles.

Since 1887, dinosaurs have been divided into two groups based on the structure of their hips. Saurischian dinosaurs had hips shaped like those of modern lizards. Ornithischian dinosaurs had hips shaped like those of modern birds.

Triceratops is one of the ornithischian dinosaurs, whose hip bones (inset) are shaped like those of modern birds.

Tyrannosaurus is in the saurischian group of dinosaurs, whose hip bones (inset) are shaped like those of modern lizards.

There are two main groups of saurischians. One group is sauropodomorphs. This group includes sauropods, such as Brachiosaurus. Sauropods ate plants and were quadrupedal, meaning they walked on four legs. The other group of saurischians, theropods, includes bipedal meat-eating predators. Some paleontologists believe birds are a branch of theropod dinosaurs.

Ornithischians are all plant eaters. They are divided into three groups. Thyreophorans include the quadrupedal stegosaurians, including Stegosaurus, and ankylosaurians, including Ankylosaurus. The other two groups are ornithopods, which include Edmontosaurus and marginocephalians.

A Dinosaur's Family Tree

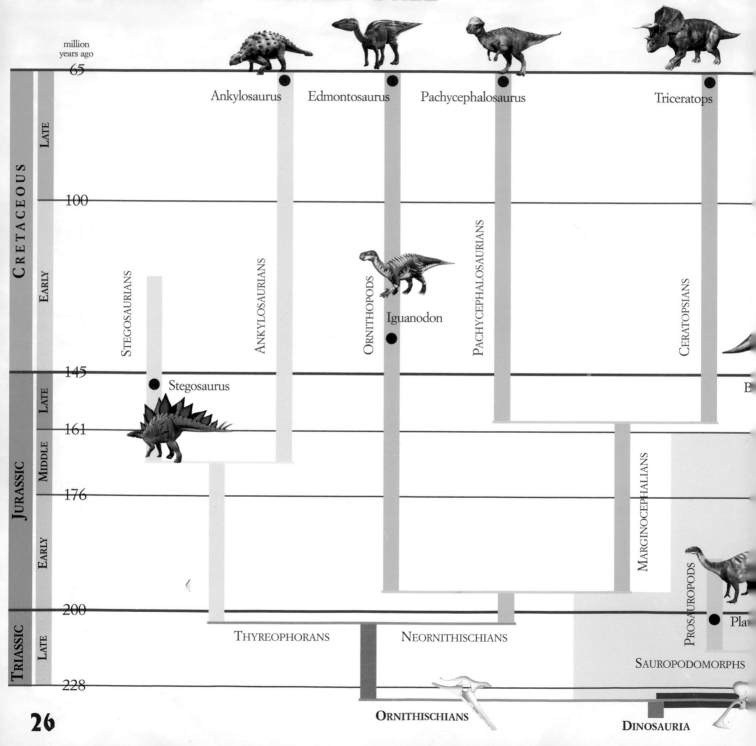

million years ago

CRETACEOUS

LATE

Ankylosaurus
Edmontosaurus
Pachycephalosaurus
Triceratops

65

100

EARLY

STEGOSAURIANS

ANKYLOSAURIANS

ORNITHOPODS

Iguanodon

PACHYCEPHALOSAURIANS

CERATOPSIANS

145

Stegosaurus

JURASSIC

LATE

161

MIDDLE

176

MARGINOCEPHALIANS

EARLY

PROSAUROPODS

Pla

200

THYREOPHORANS

NEORNITHISCHIANS

SAUROPODOMORPHS

TRIASSIC

LATE

228

26

ORNITHISCHIANS

DINOSAURIA

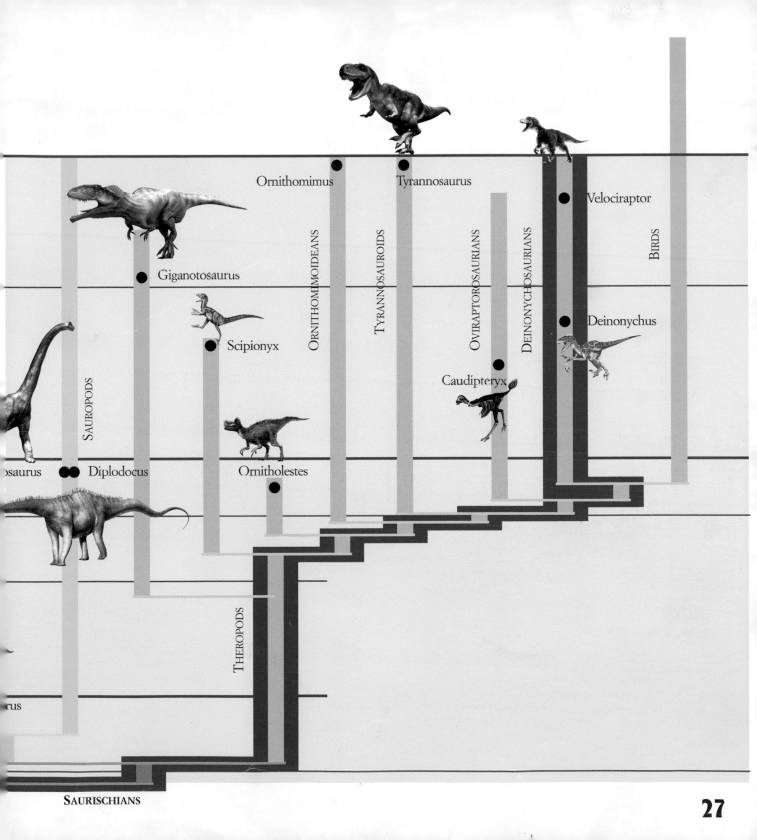

Ornithomimus

Tyrannosaurus

ORNITHOMIMOIDEANS

TYRANNOSAUROIDS

OVIRAPTOROSAURIANS

DEINONYCHOSAURIANS

BIRDS

Velociraptor

Giganotosaurus

Scipionyx

Deinonychus

SAUROPODS

Caudipteryx

osaurus ●● Diplodocus

Ornitholestes

THEROPODS

rus

SAURISCHIANS

27

GLOSSARY

Bipedal moving on two feet

Caudal related to the tail

Cervical related to the neck

Claws sharp, pointed nails on the fingers and toes of predators

Cretaceous period the period of geological time between 144 and 65 million years ago

Dorsal related to the back

Evolution changes in living things over time

Femur thigh bone

Fossil part of a living thing, such as a skeleton or leaf imprint, that has been preserved in Earth's crust from an earlier geological age

Jurassic period the period of geological time between 206 and 144 million years ago

Mesozoic era the period of geological time between 228 and 65 million years ago

Meteorite a piece of iron or rock that falls to Earth from space

Orbit the opening in the skull surrounding the eye

Paleontologist a scientist who studies prehistoric life

Predator an animal that hunts other animals for food

Prey an animal that is hunted by other animals for food

Quadrupedal moving on four feet

Skeleton the structure of an animal body, made up of bones

Skull the bones that form the head and face

Tibia shinbone

Triassic period the period of geological time between 248 and 206 million years ago

Vertebra a bone of the spine

For More Information

Books

Elaine Landau, *Velociraptor.* Danbury, CT: Children's Press, 2007.

Carol K. Lindeen, *Velociraptor.* Mankato, MN: Capstone Press, 2006.

Virginia Schomp, *Velociraptor and Other Small, Speedy Meat-Eaters.* New York: Benchmark Books/Marshall Cavendish, 2003.

Web Sites

Dinosaur Guide
http://dsc.discovery.com/guides/dinosaur/dinosaur.html
This Discovery Channel site features a richly illustrated Dinosaur Gallery that includes Velociraptor.

Prehistoric Life
http://www.bbc.co.uk/sn/prehistoric_life/
This section of the BBC Web site contains a great deal of information about dinosaurs, including galleries of illustrations along with games and quizzes.

The Smithsonian National Museum of Natural History
http://www.nmnh.si.edu/paleo/dino/
A virtual tour of the Smithsonian's National Museum of Natural History dinosaur exhibits.

ABOUT THE AUTHOR

Fabio Marco Dalla Vecchia is the curator of the Paleontological Museum of Monfalcone in Gorizia, Italy. He has participated in several paleontological field works in Italy and other countries and has directed paleontological excavations in Italy. He is the author of more than 50 scientific articles that have been published in national and international journals.

INDEX

Index